Contents

Note to Parents and Teachers

This book answers basic questions kids ask about their senses. Even if they don't know what the word "senses" means, their questions express their curiosity: "How come salt tastes…salty?" "Why do feathers tickle?" Sound familiar? You may have wondered about these things yourself once upon a time—and maybe still do.

Here, young readers will learn, in easy-to-understand language and through simple experiments and activities, some fascinating facts about their senses in a way that will start them thinking. Just don't be surprised when they come up with even more questions. As in life, there are always more questions than answers, and this book is just a beginning.

Stumped by new "sense" questions? Join in experiencing again a child's thrill of discovery by searching out answers. On the way, you and your child will learn lots of interesting new things about the senses that connect us to the world around us, and very likely about each other.

Safety First: These activities are planned to be safe and as simple as possible. Still, we strongly recommend adult supervision and ready help with all activities, especially so in a kitchen environment. Also, we suggest reviewing the **Be Safe** checklist here together with the child before starting any experiment.

First Science Experiments
SUPER SENSES

by Shar Levine and Leslie Johnstone
illustrations by Steve Harpster

Sterling Publishing Co., Inc.

C152841207

To Flo, Gail, Anne, Michael, and Stan, Nice to finally meet you.—SL

*To my friends Teresa and Dan Wilson and
their children, Conrad and Sarah.—LJ*

Edited by Claire Bazinet

Library of Congress Cataloging-in-Publication Data

Levine, Shar, 1953–
  Super senses / Shar Levine and Leslie Johnstone ; illustrated by Steve Harpster.
      p. cm. — (First science experiments)
Includes index.
Summary: Explains the senses and provides simple activities and experiments designed to show how they work.
  ISBN 0-8069-7247-5
  1. Senses and sensation—Juvenile literature. 2. Senses and sensation—Experiments—Juvenile literature. [1. Senses and sensation—Experiments. 2. Experiments.] I. Johnstone, Leslie. II. Harpster, Steve, ill. III. Title. IV. Series: First science experiments (Sterling Publishing)
QP434 .L485 2003
612.8—dc21

                                        2002015331

10 9 8 7 6 5 4 3 2 1

Published in paperback in 2005 by Sterling Publishing Co., Inc.
387 Park Avenue South, New York, N.Y. 10016
© 2003 by Shar Levine and Leslie Johnstone
Distributed in Canada by Sterling Publishing
℅ Canadian Manda Group, 165 Dufferin Street,
Toronto, Ontario, Canada M6K 3H6
Distributed in Great Britain and Europe by Chris Lloyd
at Orca Book Services, Stanley House, Fleets Lane,
Poole, BH15 3AJ, England
Distributed in Australia by Capricorn Link (Australia)
Pty. Ltd. P.O. Box 704, Windsor, NSW 2756 Australia
Printed in China
All rights reserved

Sterling ISBN 0-8069-7247-5 Hardcover
        ISBN 1-4027-2767-4 Paperback

For information about custom editions, special sales, premium and corporate purchases, please contact Sterling Special Sales Department at 800-805-5489 or specialsales@sterlingpub.com.

Be Safe

DO

- ✔ Before starting, ask an adult if it is okay to do the experiment.
- ✔ Read through each experiment with an adult first.
- ✔ If you have allergies, let a parent decide which experiments you can do.
- ✔ Have an adult handle anything made of glass, or that is sharp.
- ✔ Keep babies and pets away from experiments and supplies.
- ✔ Keep your work area clean. Wipe up all spills right away.
- ✔ Wash your hands when you are finished experimenting.
- ✔ Be careful all the time—no matter what you are doing.
- ✔ Tell an adult right away, if you or anyone gets hurt!

DON'T

- ✔ Don't put anything in your mouth, unless it's part of the experiment or an adult says it's okay to do.
- ✔ Never look directly at the sun. Strong light can hurt your eyes.

Introduction

Where are you? How do you know? Look around. You are using the sense of sight. Now, close your eyes. What do you hear? A TV playing nearby? Car horns outside? With your eyes closed, your ears tell you what's going on and where you are. You can hear, another sense.

Sniff the air. Mmmm, someone's baking cookies. You know this because of your sense of smell. What's that on your arm? You don't need to look. Your sense of touch tells you it's the cold, wet nose of your dog, wondering why you are being so quiet.

You open your eyes and see a glass of milk. You take a drink. Ahhh, the milk is cool and creamy on your tongue. You can't wait to taste those cookies, too.

That was easy. You used your eyes, ears, nose, skin, and tongue— and you know where you are and what you are doing. But, where do senses come from?

Each one of us is made up of thousands of tiny **cells** that are too small to see. But groups of cells come together to make **tissues**, and when different kinds of tissues work together to do a job, they are called **organs**.

Certain organs in our bodies allow us to sense things about the world around us—to see, hear, touch, smell, and taste. They are called **sensory organs**. The messages they send to our brains are decoded so that we can do things—like catch a ball that someone throws (sight) or find the ice-cream truck (hearing).

Sight

Did you ever wake up at night in a dark room? If there's no light, you can't see anything. If there's some light, you can see a little—but things look different. You can't see colors.

Why does that happen? There are special cells at the back of your eyeballs—**rod** cells detect light and **cone** cells detect color. When there's only a little light, the rod cells take over. That's why you see only shapes, not colors.

Light is the secret to seeing. It bounces off objects and into the eye. Look at your eyes in a mirror. See the colored ring in each eye? That colored part of your eye is called the **iris**. The black dot in the middle is called the **pupil**. The pupil isn't really a dot, but a hole that lets the light go deep into the eye.

The iris protects the inside of the eye. If you look at a bright light, the iris makes the pupil smaller, so less light comes in. When it is dark, the iris opens up to let more light in the pupil.

Do you want to know more about the eye? Look here. When light enters the eye through the pupil, it goes through a watery pocket. At the other side, an elastic window called a **lens** stretches across the eyeball like a tiny drum. This lens not only bends the light, but it turns it upside down!

Finally, the light hits the **retina**, that layer of detector cells at the back of the eyeball that are shaped like rods and cones. When light hits the cells, they send a message to the brain through the **optic nerve**. Your eyes see the outside world upside down. When your brain receives the message, it turns everything right side up again—and what you see makes sense.

How the eye sees:
Light bounces off the tree and into the eye through the pupil. The lens turns the light upside down.

Why do some people wear glasses

You can't see inside your eyes, but let's do an experiment and find out what's going on.

You need

- adult helper
- clear drinking glass
- clear plastic wrap
- rubber band or tape
- water
- spoon
- a coin or small toy

Do this

1 Put the small toy or coin into the drinking glass.

2 Put a piece of clear wrap over the top of the glass. Fix it on with a rubber band or tape. The wrap should sag just a little.

3 Using the spoon, fill the plastic wrap "pocket" with water.

4 Look down through the water at the toy in the glass. Now, look at it through the side of the glass.

What happened?

The coin or toy looked bigger from the top. The water made an upside-down dome shape called a **convex** lens. Like the lens in your eye, your water lens bends light. It happens because light moves more slowly through water than through air. Look through a convex lens, like the side of a round fishbowl, and things look bigger. People wear eyeglasses with convex lenses to help them read. By bending the light, they bring the words on the page closer.

   Sometimes people have trouble seeing far away. Their eyes don't **focus**, or adjust, from far to near. Everything looks fuzzy, so they wear eyeglasses to bring the world into focus, and see things more clearly.

what is a blind spot?

Cover one eye with your hand. Can you still see, out of your other eye? Yes, but you aren't seeing everything. Remember those optic nerves that carry messages from your eyes? The place where they attach to your eyes is called a **blind spot**. Now let's see why.

You need

◆ the star and square picture below

Do this

1 Cover your left eye. With your head close to the book *look at the red star* with your *right* eye. (You should be able to see the blue square, too.)

2 Keep looking at the star, and very slowly move your head away from the book. Stop when you can't see the square anymore. The book will be about 3 inches (7.5 cm) from the tip of your nose. (If you move your head farther away, you should be able to see the square again.)

3 Next, cover your right eye. With your head close to the book, this time *look at the blue square* with your *left* eye. (You should be able to see the star, too.)

4 Keep looking at the square, and very slowly move your head away from the book. Stop when you can't see the red star anymore.

What happened?

As you moved your head back, the blue square disappeared. After you changed eyes, the red star disappeared.

Each eyeball has a blind spot. Light bounces off the square and the star. It goes into the eye and hits the retina. But, that place on the retina is where the optic nerve connects. There's no room for the rod and the cone cells that detect the light—so nothing can be seen. In each eye, it's as if you were blind in just that one spot.

Can my eyes play other tricks on me?

Sometimes the eyes and the brain can fool you. Your eyes may see something, but your brain doesn't. Let's take something as plain as the nose on your face—your nose. Look at your nose, right now. See it? Now, look down at your feet. Your nose disappears! You know it's still there on your face, but your brain ignores it.

Now it's your turn to trick your brain. You know all your colors, don't you? You can tell pink from blue? Let's see what happens when the colors are hidden in words.

You need

◆ this list of words

PINK **YELLOW** BLACK **BLUE** GRAY

GREEN RED **ORANGE** PURPLE **BROWN**

Do this

1 Look at the list of words, but *don't* read the words. Instead, say the *color* the words are printed in.

What happened?

I'll bet it was easy at first, but then you slowed down and began to make mistakes. It probably surprised you, because you know your colors. So, why did that happen? Your brain started to mix up the *color* of the word with the *meaning* of the word. Yes, reading the name of a color in a different color can get your poor brain so confused!

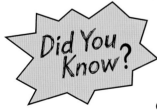

Crossing your eyes is good for you. The muscles that turn your eyeballs so you can see left, right, up, and down get a good workout when you cross your eyes.

Hearing

Is there a cat, dog, or horse nearby? Watch its ears and make a small noise. Don't you wish your ears could go up, down, and back and forth like that? Some people can "wiggle" their ears, but only a little. Human ears pretty much stay put, but they are shaped to capture sound out of the air.

Once the sounds enter the ear, they move down a tube-shaped opening called the **ear canal**. At the bottom, the sounds bounce off the **eardrum**. The eardrum vibrates, or shakes, and pushes three tiny bones inside your ear against a fluid-filled tube with hairlike detector cells. The sound messages travel from the sensors to your brain…and you hear!

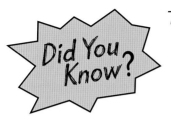

The three tiny bones in your ears that help you to hear have names. They are called the anvil, the hammer, and the stirrup, because that is what they look like.

The anvil looks like the big metal "T"-shape, called an anvil, that a blacksmith works on to make horseshoes. The hammer looks like a small hammer. And the stirrup looks like the part of a saddle that holds your foot when you're on a horse.

Now, here's a tip. If anyone should try to stump you by asking, "Of the 206 bones in the human body, which is the smallest?" answer "the stirrup," and you would be right!

If my eyes can fool me, can my ears fool me, too?

When things are quiet—with no music or television playing—sit down, close your eyes, and just listen. What do you hear? A barking dog sounds very different from a closing door. But how hard is it to tell some sounds apart? Let's see.

You need

- a chair
- a helper
- sound-makers (see list)

Do this

1. Ask your helper to sit in the chair and listen. From behind the chair (out of sight), make some sounds from the following list or try some of your own. Ask your helper what you did to make the sound.

- ✔ rub your hands together
- ✔ tear a sheet of paper
- ✔ pour water into a bowl

✔ "slam" a book closed
✔ tap on a table
✔ run a finger along a comb
✔ shake a box of paper clips
✔ bounce a ball
✔ ring a bell

✔ step on some bubble wrap
✔ "pop" an air-filled
   paper bag
✔ knock down some blocks
✔ rub sandpaper against wood
✔ "plunk" a rubber band

What happened?

Did your helper get some wrong? Don't be surprised. Many sounds are a lot alike.

In movies, sounds like thunder and the wind are "made up." They're only **sound effects**. You expect to hear the sounds, so your mind believes the fake ones are real. Take dinosaurs, for example. Dinosaurs lived so long ago, nobody really knows what they sounded like. Sound people, who work on movies, just make sounds up—and you really think you're hearing a dinosaur roar.

MEOW

Why do we have two ears ?

The game Marco Polo is usually played in a swimming pool. One person is "it" and moves around with eyes closed, calling out "Marco." The other players answer "Polo" so "it" can try to find and tag one of them. Two ears are a great help in this game. Why? Let's see.

You need

◆ a helper ◆ a chair ◆ a quiet room

Do this

1 Ask your helper to sit quietly with eyes closed and listen. Explain that you will make some sounds. Your helper should point toward the sounds you make.

2 First, move to one side of your helper. Softly clap your hands. Then, move quietly to the other side and clap again. Move farther away, to other places in the room. Clap each time. Is your helper following the sounds?

3 Now, ask your helper, with eyes still shut, to cover one ear tightly with a hand. Move around and clap softly again in several places. Watch where your helper points now.

4 Then ask your helper to change hands, and cover the other ear tightly. Again, move around the room and clap softly.

What happened?

When you were very close and your helper listened with both ears, he or she could probably tell where the sound was coming from. As you moved farther away and your helper listened with only one ear at a time, it was harder to find you. We can tell direction when we use both ears because of the difference in the sound coming into each ear. When we only hear through one ear, it becomes much more difficult to tell the location of the sound.

Why shouldn't I poke things in my ears ?

Did you know you have a set of drums? Not bongo, congo, or kettle drums, but eardrums. They're not good for pounding out a beat, but eardrums are great for hearing your favorite band—or a fire-engine siren.

Every sound you hear is caused by **vibrations** or waves. Your eardrums catch the sound waves that ride the air into your ears. This starts three very small bones in your ear vibrating, too. That's when hair-like detector cells in the ear, in a long tube called the **cochlea**, send the sound signals to your brain. Let's see how the eardrums do their work.

You need
- plastic garbage bag
- large metal bowl
- ruler
- crayon
- scissors
- masking tape
- salt

Do this

1 Lay the garbage bag flat on a table. Put the bowl upside down on top of the bag.

2 On the bag, draw a big circle about 2 inches (5 cm) out from the bowl. Cut out the circle you drew on the top layer.

3 Turn the bowl over and put the plastic circle over it. Tape it to the bowl, all around. Stretch the plastic a little to make it a "tight" drum.

4 Put a little salt in the middle of the plastic. Make loud noises near the drum and watch what happens to the salt.

What happened?

The salt moved! The top of your bowl drum vibrated, or shook. It detected sound waves—just like your eardrums do. But what if you made a hole in the bowl drum? It wouldn't work. Like a broken drum, your eardrums can be damaged, too. That's why you should never, ever, poke things in your ears. Your ears can even be hurt by loud noises—so you sometimes cover your ears with your hands to protect them.

Touch

What if you couldn't feel things? Even putting on eyeglasses or drinking water would be very hard to do.

You get your sense of touch from the skin. Your skin is the largest organ in your body. (Yes, it's made up of different kinds of cells working together, so it's an organ.) Skin is amazing. It is very thin, but it covers all of you—from your head to your toes. It moves any way you do, and it is waterproof. It's your first protection from the sun, dirt and germs, and other things that might hurt you.

Your skin is made up of two layers. The top part you see is called the **epidermis**. Underneath is a layer called the **dermis**. The dermis has sensor cells that detect pain, pressure, heat, and cold. They are always sending messages to your brain so you can figure out, "What *is* that touching me?"

Try this ➤ Sit down together with a friend and take off your shoes and socks. Now, gently tickle the bottoms of your friend's feet one at a time. Have your friend try the same thing on your feet. Did you both laugh when your feet were tickled? Now, try tickling your own feet. Did you laugh this time?

As it turns out, you can't tickle yourself. Scientists think that is because you not only know what's going to happen, you are in control of what is happening. So your brain tells your body that it is not being tickled.

Why do things feel hot and cold at the same time ?

Do you feel the bathtub water before you get in, to see if it's too hot or too cold? Sometimes, it feels fine on your hand, but too hot when you step in. That's strange. Did the water temperature change? What is going on? Let's see.

You need

- three deep bowls
- ice water
- warm water
- room temperature water

Do this

1. Fill a bowl half full of ice water. Fill another bowl half full of warm water. Fill a third bowl half full of room temperature water.

2 Place your left hand in the ice water and your right hand in the warm water. Count slowly to ten.

3 Take your hands out of the water and put them both in the bowl of room temperature water. Does the water temperature feel the same to both hands?

4 Try it again. This time place your right hand in the ice water and your left hand in the warm water. How does the room temperature water feel now?

What happened?

The room temperature water felt warm to the hand that had been in the ice water and cool to the hand that had been in the warm water.

Your skin cells can tell if they are "getting warmer" or "getting colder," but they can't measure the exact temperature. So when your feet are cold from standing on the cool bathroom floor, the bath water will feel "hotter" to your feet than it feels on your warmer hands, even though the temperature of the bath water doesn't change.

Can I tell what things are without seeing them ?

Did you hear the story about the blind men and the elephant? One blind man is holding the elephant's trunk. "An elephant is like a fire hose. Long and thick." The second man is feeling one of the elephant's legs. "No, it's like a tree trunk. Thick and bumpy." The third man is feeling the elephant's tail. "You're wrong. It's like a long rope with a tassel on the end." The moral of the story is, you can't always rely on just your sense of touch to tell you about the world you live in.

There isn't an elephant in this activity, but let's see if you can fool yourself and your friends.

You need

- ◆ 2 marbles
- ◆ 2 dice
- ◆ 2 cotton balls
- ◆ 2 lemons
- ◆ 2 each of other small things
- ◆ 2 small paper bags

Do this

1 Place one marble, one of the dice, one cotton ball, and one lemon into a paper bag. Place the other of the same object into another paper bag. (If you don't have two of each of these items, you can use two of any other small object that is safe to touch.)

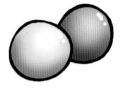

2 Reach your left hand into one bag and your right into the other bag. Without looking inside the bags, can you take out the two marbles?

3 Try to match up the other objects.

What happened?

You can match up the pairs because they feel the same. The marbles feel heavy, smooth, round, and hard. Nothing else feels like the marbles. Things have different weights and shapes, and feel different—hard, soft, smooth, bumpy, round, square. Each difference is a clue telling the skin on your fingertips what is the same and what is different.

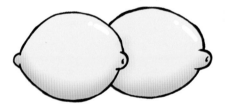

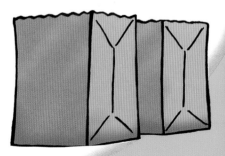

How do blind people read ?

Close your eyes and try to read the words on this page. You couldn't read a thing, could you? Blind people may not have the sense of sight, but they have learned to use other senses to tell them about the world around them.

You'd be surprised just how sensitive the tips of your fingers can be. They can even help you learn to read.

You need
- index cards
- soft surface (computer mouse pad)
- sharp pencil

Do this

1. Put an index card down on a mouse pad. Press down on the card with the tip of the pencil.

2. Turn the card over. Feel the bump? Put it aside.

3 Now, take another card, and make two bumps near each other.

4 Turn the card over and feel again. Can you feel two bumps, not one? If you can't feel two separate bumps, try again. Make the bumps just a little farther apart. Now feel them.

What happened?

You could easily feel one bump. That one bump is the letter **a** in **braille**, an alphabet used by people who can't see. When you made two bumps a little apart, your finger could "read" that there were two bumps. Two bumps this way ⠆ is **b** in braille, and two bumps this way •• is **c** in braille. The braille alphabet is made up of groups of bumps in place of letters.

> ⠗ = **r**

In braille ⠊ ⠉⠁⠝ ⠗⠑⠁⠙ means **I can read**.

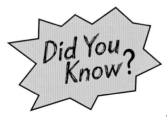

Did You Know? Some elevator cars have braille numbers near the buttons for the floors. Next time you are in an elevator, practice reading the braille with your fingertips.

Smell

Take a close look at a bug. Can you see its nose? Some insects have over 100,000 hairs on their antenna and each hair acts like a tiny nose. The sense of smell is one we share with even the simplest types of animal.

Scientists think that people can tell the difference between about 10,000 different odors. This seems pretty amazing, but it isn't as impressive as the detecting ability of the family dog, who can identify over 20,000 different odors.

When you breathe in, tiny bits of things called **chemicals** that are floating in the air enter your nose, too. When these chemicals come in contact with detector cells high up in your nose, a signal is sent to your brain. Your brain allows you to figure out what you are smelling.

The group of cells that detect odor are only about the size of a small postage stamp and they are covered with a thin layer of **mucus**. If you get a cold, this mucus gets thicker so you usually can't smell very much.

The hairs in your nose are there to help the mucus keep out dust, flying bugs, and other small things.

Can I tell what something is just by smelling it ?

Stick out your tongue. Can you smell anything with it? If you were a snake or a Gila monster, your tongue would act as a nose and pick up smells from the air. You won't need your tongue, but you will need your nose for this next activity.

You need

- a helper
- 6 small plastic containers (not see-through)
- aluminum foil
- masking tape
- pencil and paper
- 6 different "smelly" things: banana, cinnamon stick, lemon or orange peel, whole cloves, coffee beans, garlic, mint leaves, pine needles, flowers, perfume, scented oils, spices.

Do this

1. Stick masking tape on each container. Write a different number, 1 to 6, on each container.

2 Ask your helper to put something smelly into each container and cover it with foil so you can't see it.

3 When you are ready for the test, poke 4 or 5 small holes in the foil cover. You can use the pencil.

4 Put your nose near the holes and sniff. Write down the number of the container and what you think is in it.

5 Take a few breaths of fresh air. This clears your nose of the first smell. Do the same with the other samples, taking fresh breaths in between.

What happened?

If the smell was strong and came through the holes, you were probably able to tell what was inside. Sometimes you think you know a smell, but you can't put a name to it. It smells sort of like…or almost like… something else. People can smell thousands of different odors, but that doesn't mean they can name them all. Being able to identify different smells takes some practice.

How do scratch-and-sniff stickers work ?

Do you like scratch-and-sniff stickers? You use your fingernail to scratch them gently and then you smell where you scratched. They smell much stronger after you scratch than before. Why is that?

Here are some ideas for making some scratch-and-sniff cards.

You need

- ✦ index cards
- ✦ pencil
- ✦ glue
- ✦ powdered spices such as cinnamon, onion, ginger, garlic, allspice

Do this

1 Print each spice name you will use on the back of a card.

2 Spread a thin layer of glue over the front of each card. Sprinkle some of the spice, that you printed on the back, over the glue. Shake off any extra spice that doesn't stick to the glue.

3 Let the glue dry completely. Scratch the spice and try smelling it. Can you tell which spice is which?

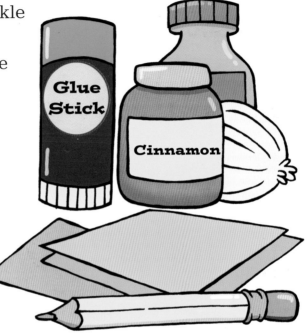

What happened?

When you scratched at the cards you made, some of the chemicals that give the spices their special odors floated into the air. This is exactly what happens with scratch-and-sniff stickers. The chemicals that make up the odors have been fixed onto the stickers. By scratching them, you release part of the chemicals. Once the chemical is in the air, it can enter your nose and be detected by those special cells in your nose when you sniff.

How good is my nose at smelling things?

Some people who can see are **color blind**. They can't tell the difference between red and green, or other colors. Some people can hear, but are **tone deaf**. They can't tell the difference between different musical notes. Now for something really strange: there are people who are **odor blind** and can't tell the difference between certain smells.

Your nose may not be as good at detecting things as your pet pooch, but just how sensitive is it?

You need

- 8 glasses or cups
- measuring cup
- water
- vinegar
- eyedropper
- measuring spoons
- vanilla extract

Do this

1 Pour half a cup of water into each glass and add vinegar as shown.

2 Starting with glass #1, sniff each glass until you can smell vinegar in the water. What number glass is it? How much vinegar is in that glass?

4 Empty the glasses. Do the experiment again, but this time use vanilla extract instead of vinegar.

What happened?

I'll bet you sniffed several glasses with vinegar in them before you could finally say, "Aha! I smell it!" When you did the same experiment using vanilla extract, you probably smelled it earlier. Vanilla extract has a stronger smell than vinegar, so it is easier for your nose to detect it, even if there is only a little bit there.

Taste

You probably think most about taste when you are eating something very good…or so very bad that you run to wash your mouth out!

Stick out your tongue and take a close look at it in a mirror. Somewhere on that wet, pink thing are groups of cells called **taste buds**. It's these taste buds that tell you if something tastes salty, sweet, bitter, or sour. They also tell you other things about foods.

Maybe you like hot pizza, but think that cold, leftover pizza is gross. When taste and smell work together, you get something called **flavor**. The flavor of food includes how it feels in your mouth and the temperature of the food. When foods are hot, the smells are stronger. Your nose takes in these stronger odors, and your brain reacts to them. This is one reason why foods taste sweeter when they are warm than when they are cold.

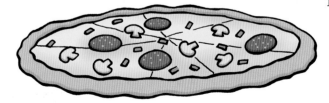

Is spicy a taste? *If you happen to eat some food that has chili pepper or hot sauce in it, your lips might burn and your tongue would hurt. "Hot" or spicy foods cause the pain sensors in your mouth to send a message to your brain.*

Chili peppers have something called **capsaicin** *in them. When you eat them, or foods with the chilies in it, the capsaicin bothers the pain sensors in your mouth. The more chilies you eat, the hotter things taste! This is why, when you eat spicy foods, you think that your mouth is on fire.*

But your brain gets really confused when you eat something with a strong minty flavor. It's "icy-hot," because your taste buds send both messages at once to your brain.

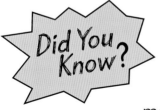

There is something you can do if you don't like hot foods and your mouth starts to burn. Pop something without much taste— like plain bread, rice, or potatoes—into your mouth. It will take some of the "heat" away.

Where are my taste buds ?

The detector cells that tell you if something is sweet, salty, sour, or bitter are in your mouth. But where? And do they work on different tastes? Let's do some detective work.

You need

- a sink
- cotton-tipped swabs
- 3 small cups
- stirrers
- baking soda
- vinegar
- salt
- sugar
- water

Do this

1. Set up everything near a sink. Take some water and swish it around your mouth. You want your mouth to be nice and clean. Swallow or spit it out.

2. Dip a clean swab into some vinegar. Touch the swab to your teeth and gums. Do you

taste the vinegar? Now touch the tip of your tongue. Can you taste vinegar there? Try touching other places in your mouth and on your tongue. When you are finished, wash your mouth out with water until you can't taste the vinegar anymore.

3 Fill a small cup with water and add a teaspoon of salt. Stir until the salt dissolves. Dip a new swab into the salt water and test the places you did in step **2**. Rinse your mouth out.

4 Do the same as in step **3** again, but put in sugar instead of salt. Next, test the places in your mouth using baking soda.

What happened?

You found your taste buds. They are all on top of your tongue. You couldn't taste anything when you touched your teeth, gums, or other places in your mouth.

The chemicals that make up the foods we eat find their way to the taste buds hidden away on the tongue.

Try this➤ Go into the kitchen for some milk. Swish it around your mouth, then swallow and look at your tongue. Those little pink dots you see are the **papillae**, the little "caves" where the taste buds are hiding.

Why don't things taste the same when I have a cold?

You sneeze a few times and your nose stuffs up. Suddenly, the things you eat don't taste the way they should. Maybe the cold germs are bothering your taste buds, too? Let's do a test.

You need

- adult helper
- lemon wedges
- lime wedges
- orange wedges
- grapefruit wedges
- pencil and paper

Do this

1. Close your eyes. Your helper will hold out small pieces of each fruit for you to smell.

2. Sniff each piece your helper holds near your nose. Can you tell what fruit it is just by the smell? Your helper will write down your guesses. How did you do?

3 After a moment's rest, close your eyes again. Gently pinch your nose closed, too, so you can't smell the fruit. This time, your helper will pass you pieces of fruit. Taste each one. (Remember to keep your eyes and nose closed.) Can you recognize the kind of fruit just from the taste?

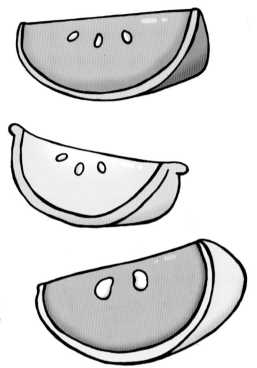

4 For the last part of the test, just close your eyes. Your helper will pass you the pieces of fruit again. You will be able to smell *and* taste it. What are the fruits now?

What happened?

Most people identify fruits from their smell. It is harder to tell what something is just from tasting it. Your sense of smell and your sense of taste work together as a team. When you pinch your nose closed, or a cold makes your nose all blocked up, food won't taste the same. But don't blame your taste buds: it's just that you can't smell it.

Can I taste color ?

What if you could change the way food looks? Would it still taste the same?

Ketchup is usually red. Now you can buy purple and green ketchup, too, but some people will only eat the red kind. Does changing the way food looks, change the way it tastes?

You need

- a helper
- colorless soda pop or white grape juice
- food coloring
- 5 clear drinking glasses
- spoon

Do this

1 Put some soda pop or juice into each drinking glass, about 1/4 full.

2 Add drops of coloring as shown, and mix well.

X

1 **2** **3** **4** **5**

3 Line up the five glasses and ask your helper to be your "taste tester." Your helper should take a sip from each glass of pop or juice and tell you something about the taste of each one.

4 Now ask your helper to close his or her eyes and take another sip from one or more of the glasses. You pick which ones. What does your helper say about it now?

What happened?

At first, your taste tester probably thought the different colored liquids tasted...different! That's because we expect things that look different to taste different. Our mind just tricks us. You can't really taste colors— only flavors. Without seeing the soda or juice, your helper couldn't tell them apart.

Index